NEW COLLECTION
Express Yourself
Swear Word
Adult Coloring Books
Vol: 2

STRESS RELIEVING
- HOTTEST NEW DESIGNS -

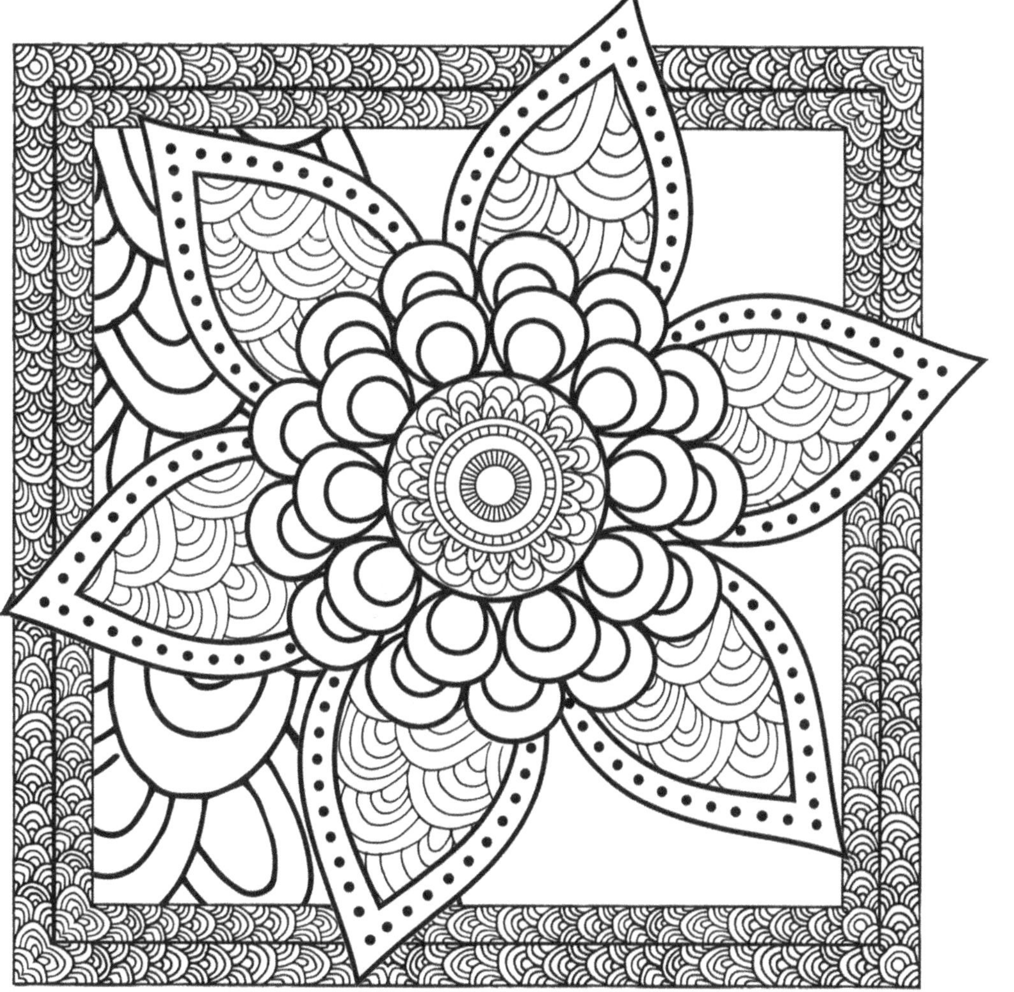

Published by:
SureShot Books Publishing LLC
P.O. Box 924
Nyack, New York 10960
www.sureshotbooks.com

PRINTED IN THE UNITED STATES OF AMERICA

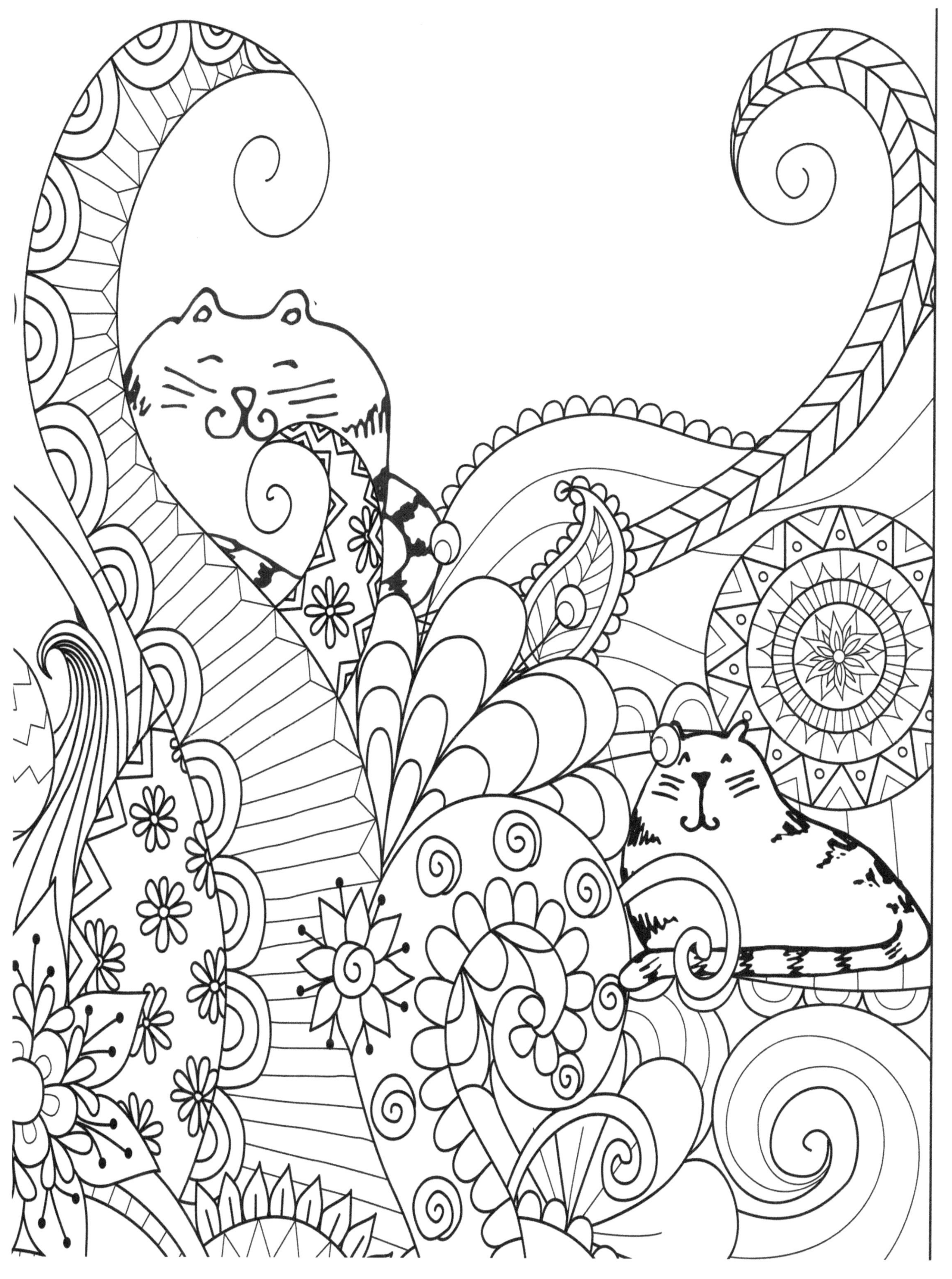

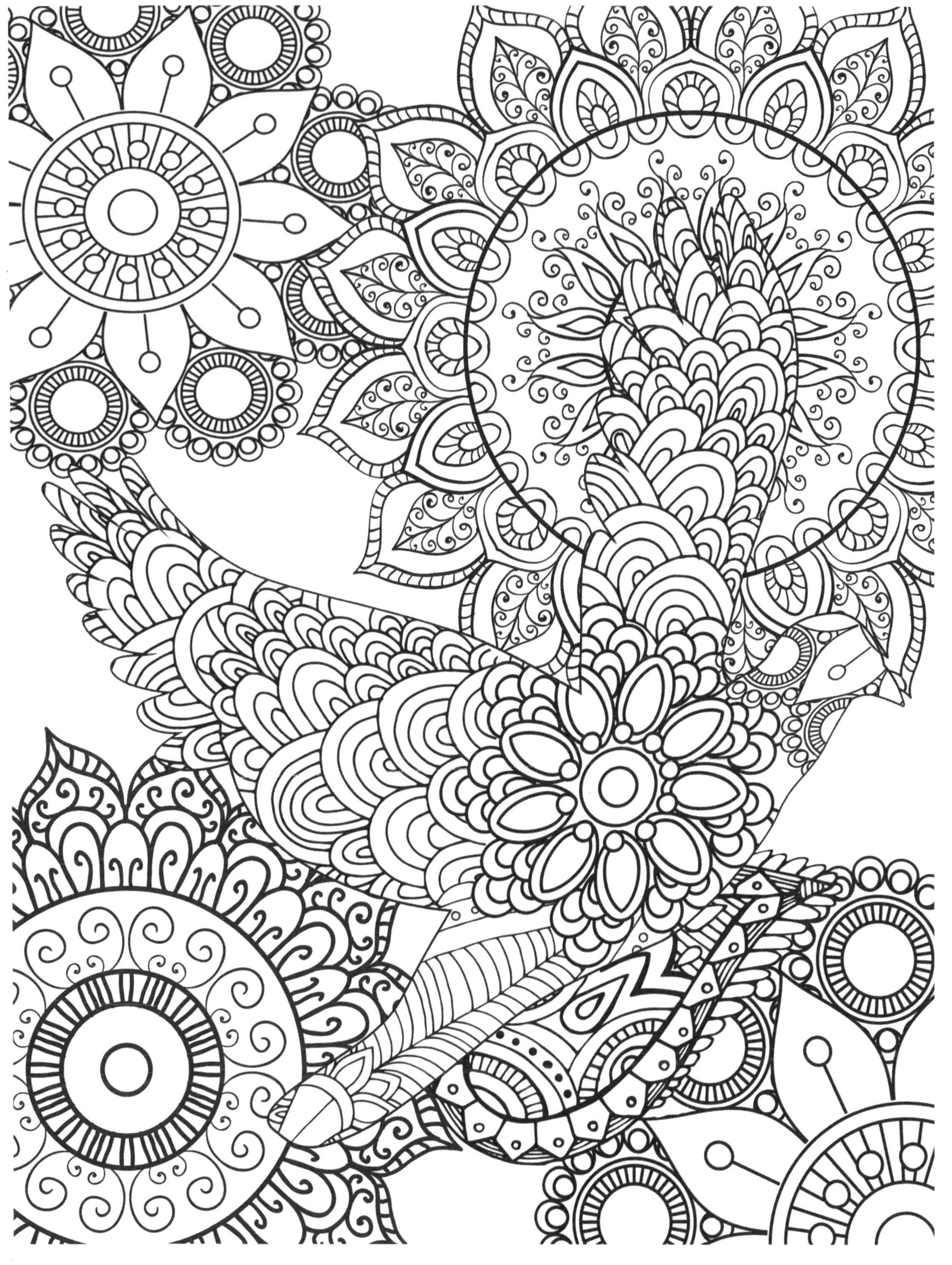

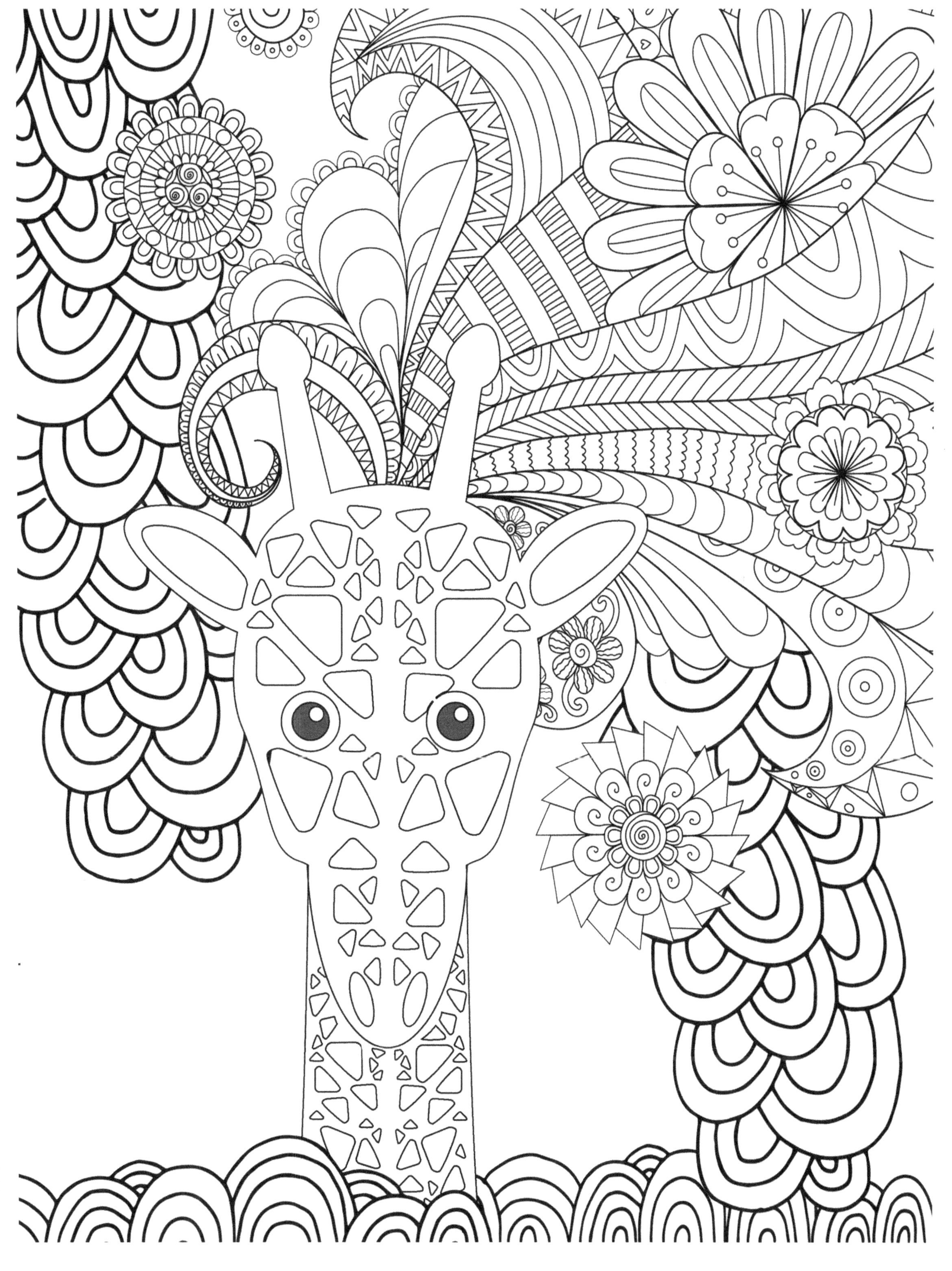

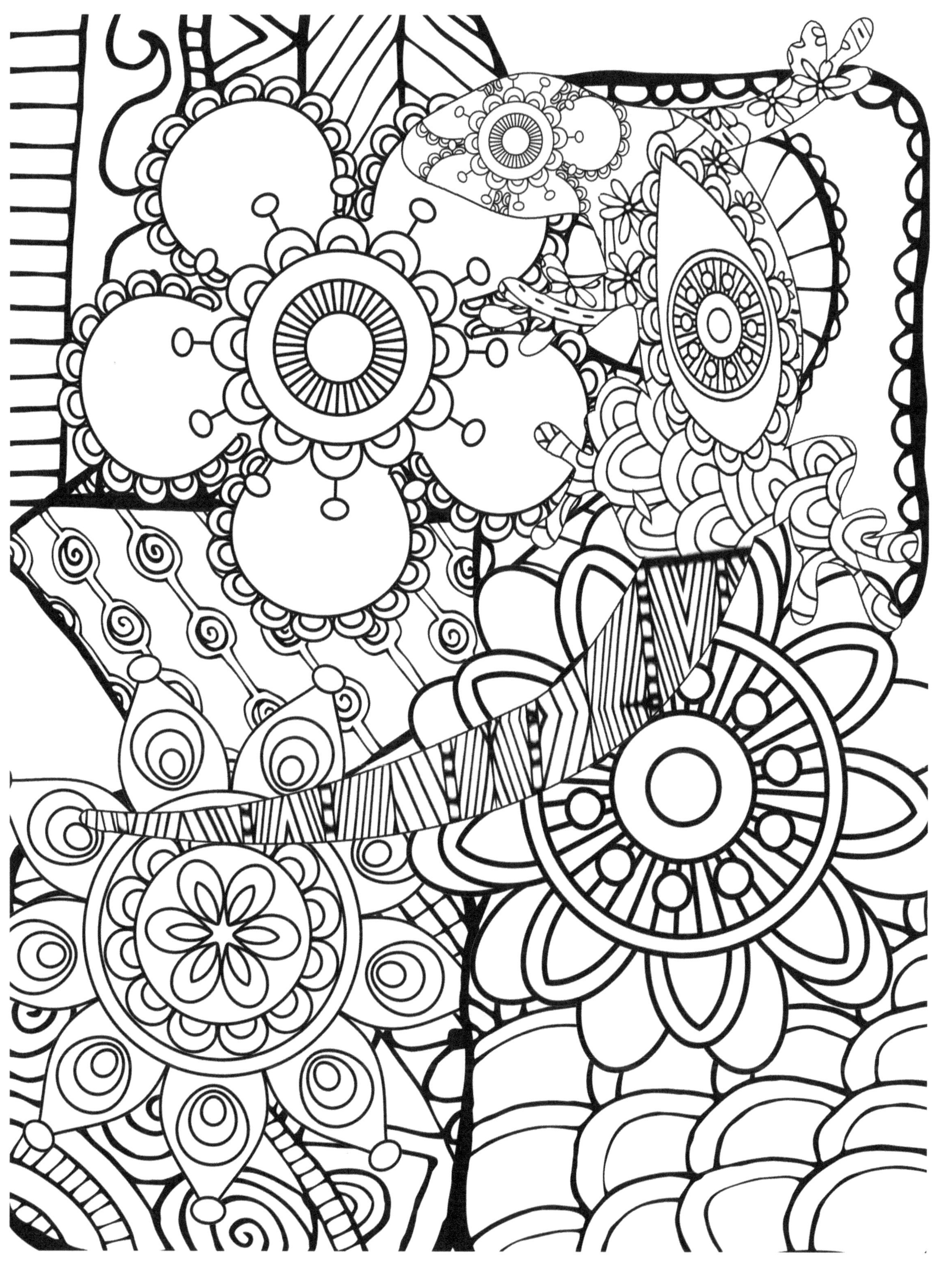

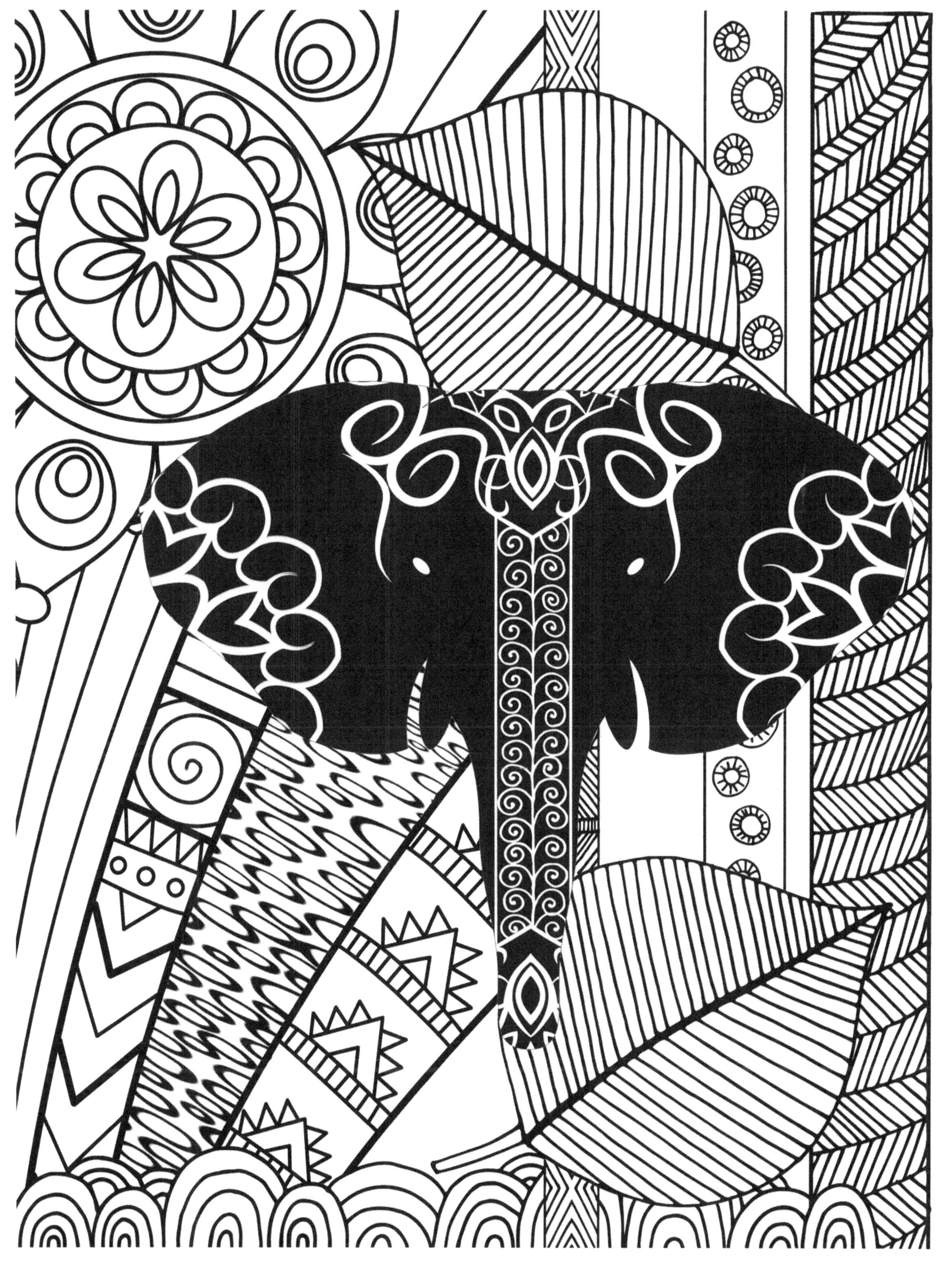

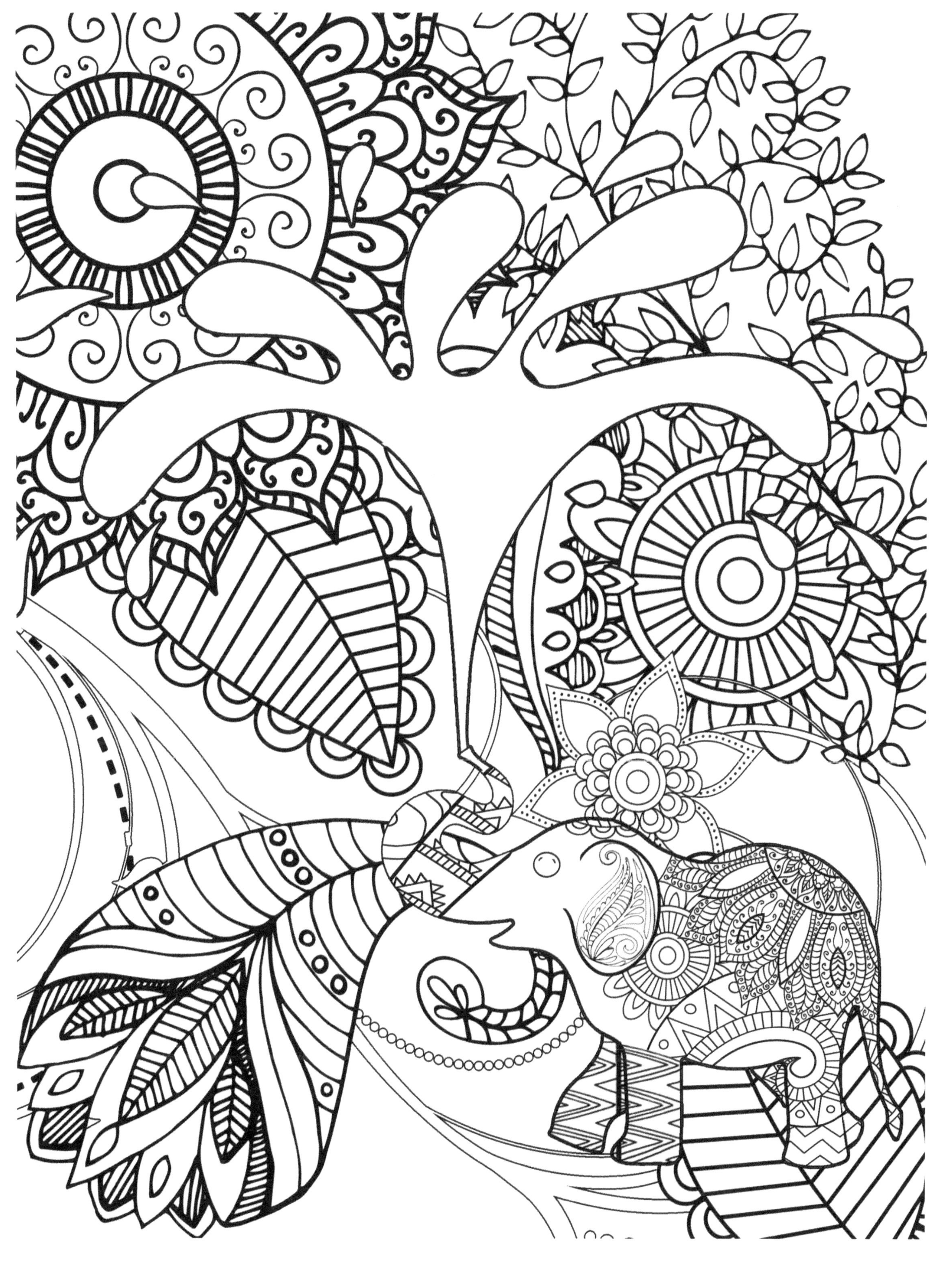

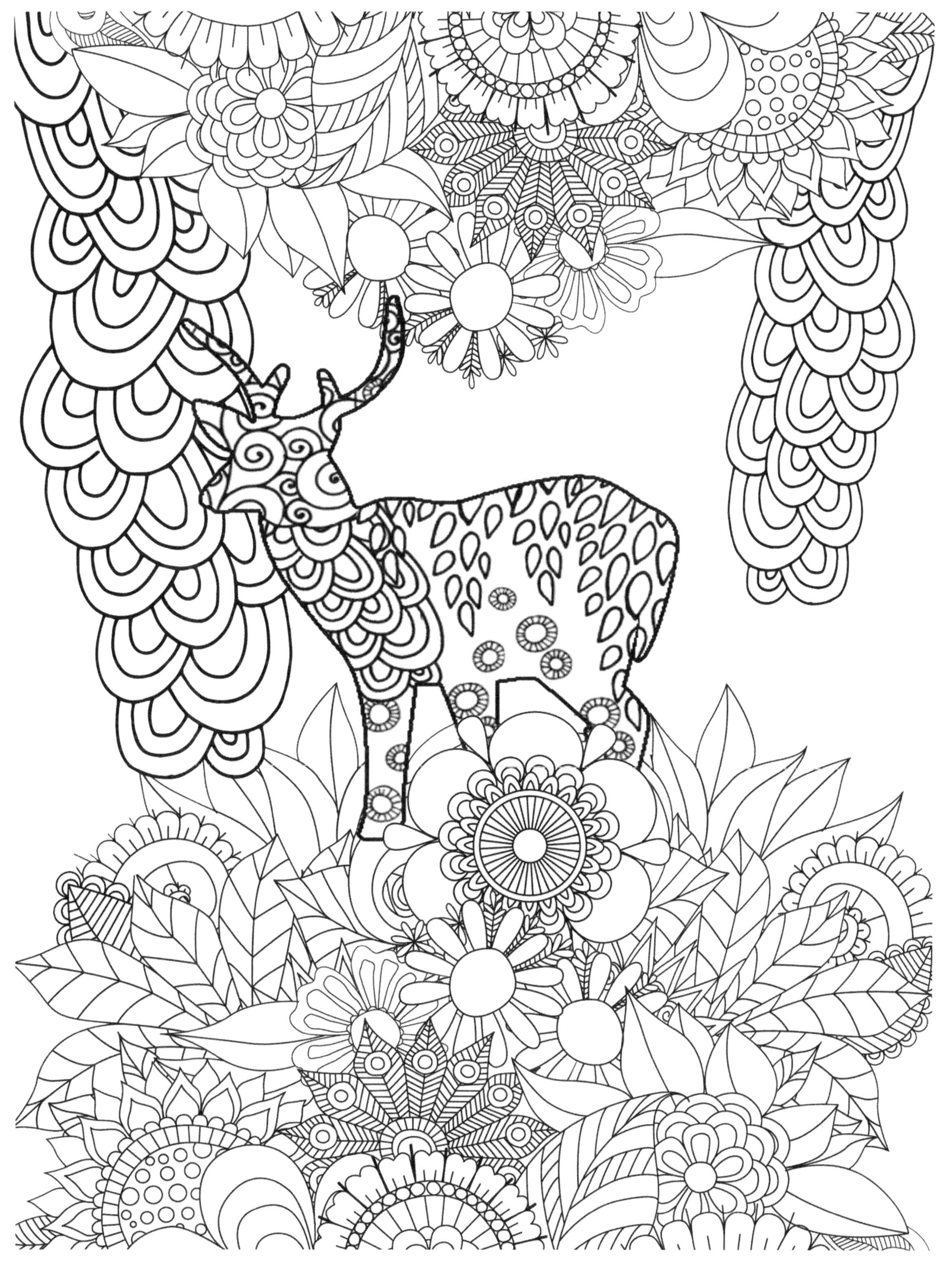

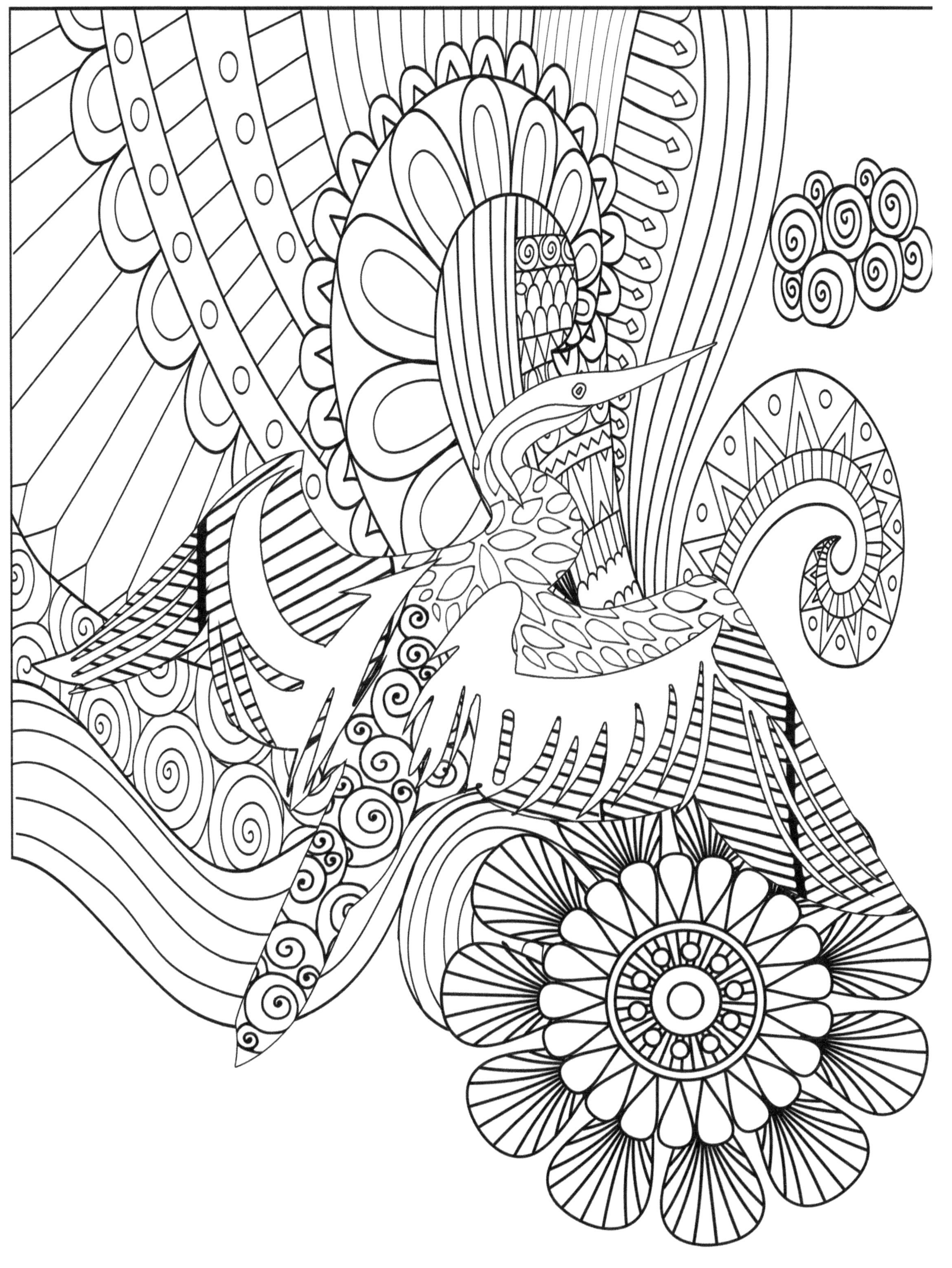

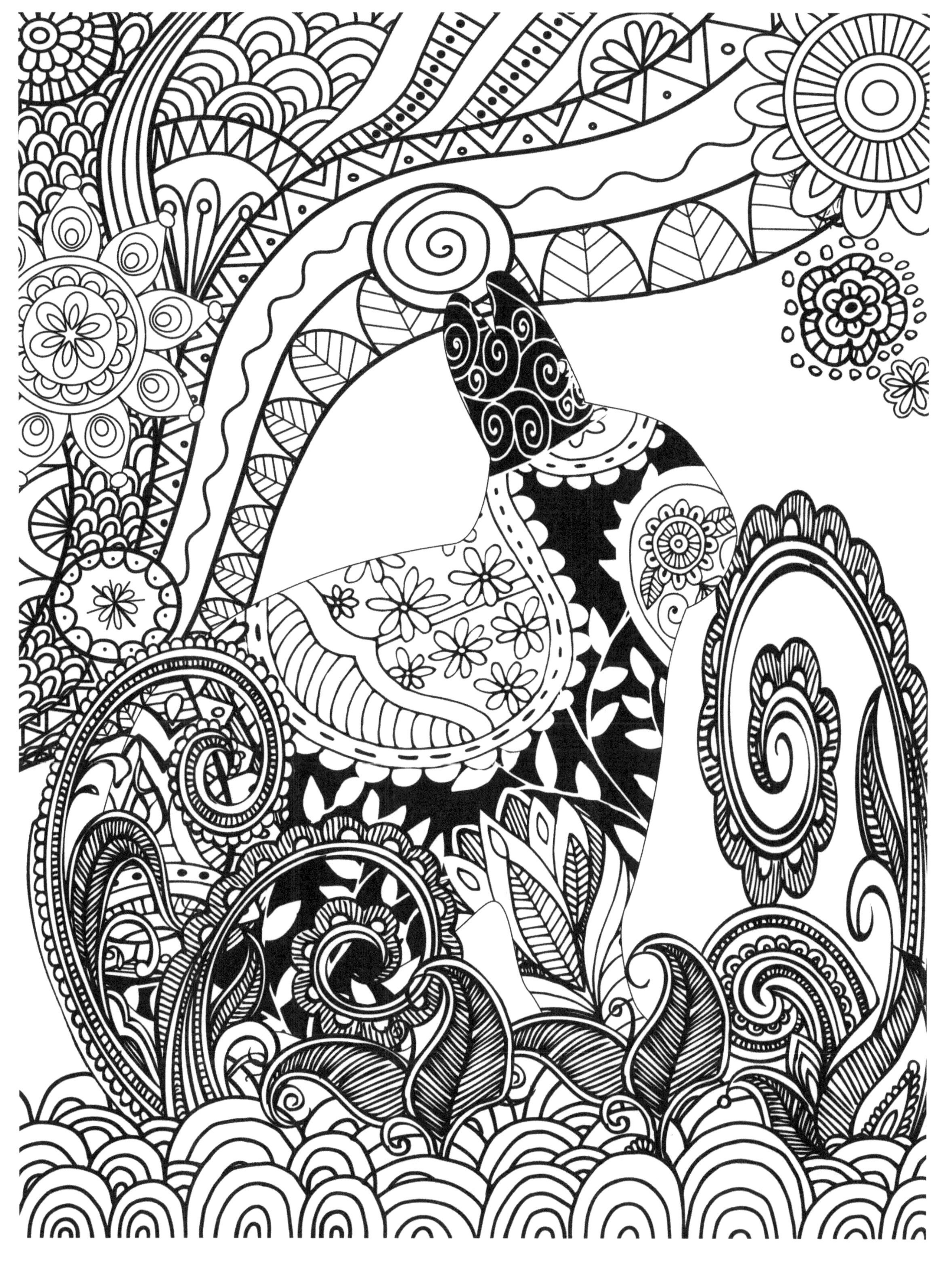

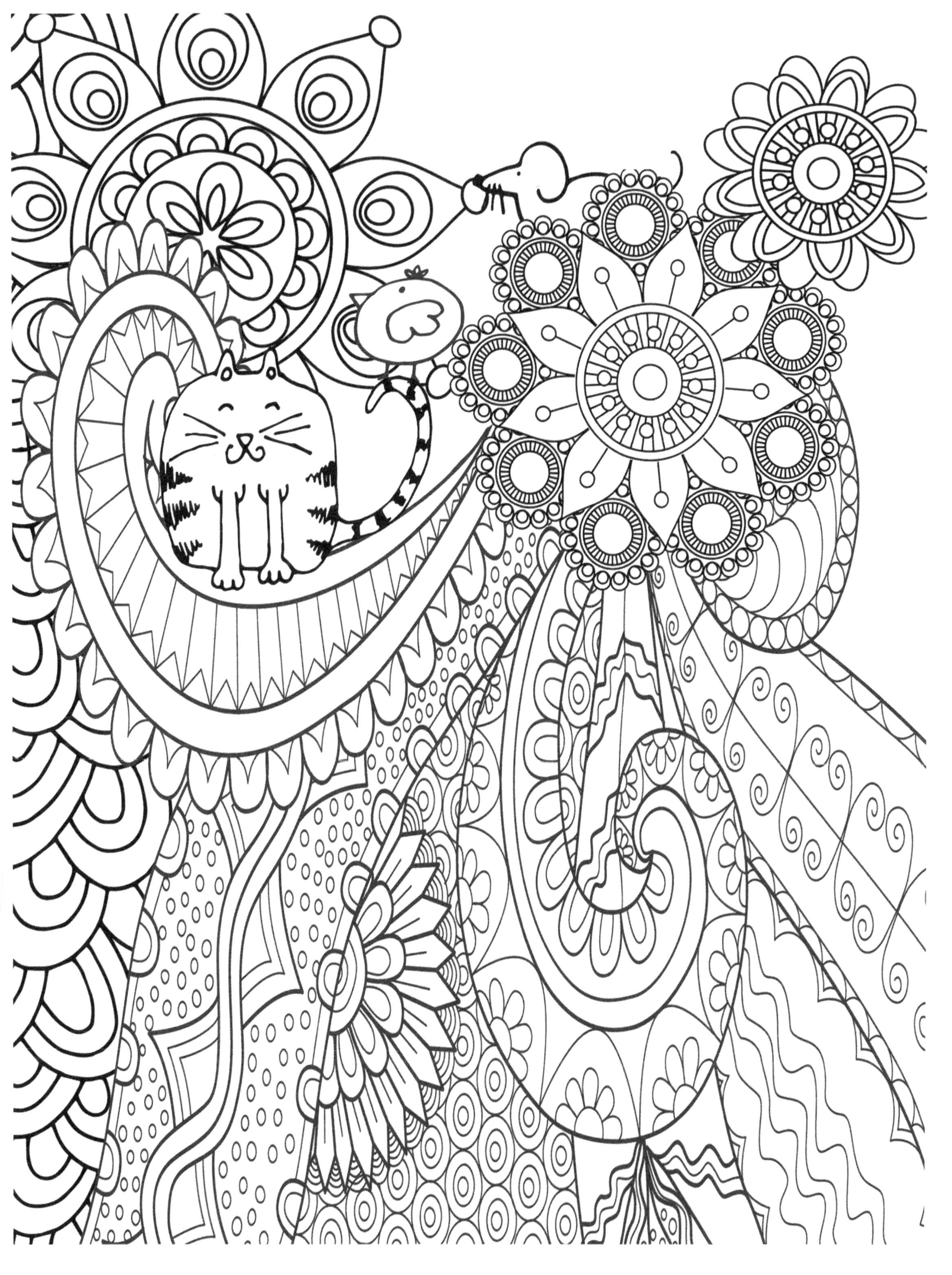

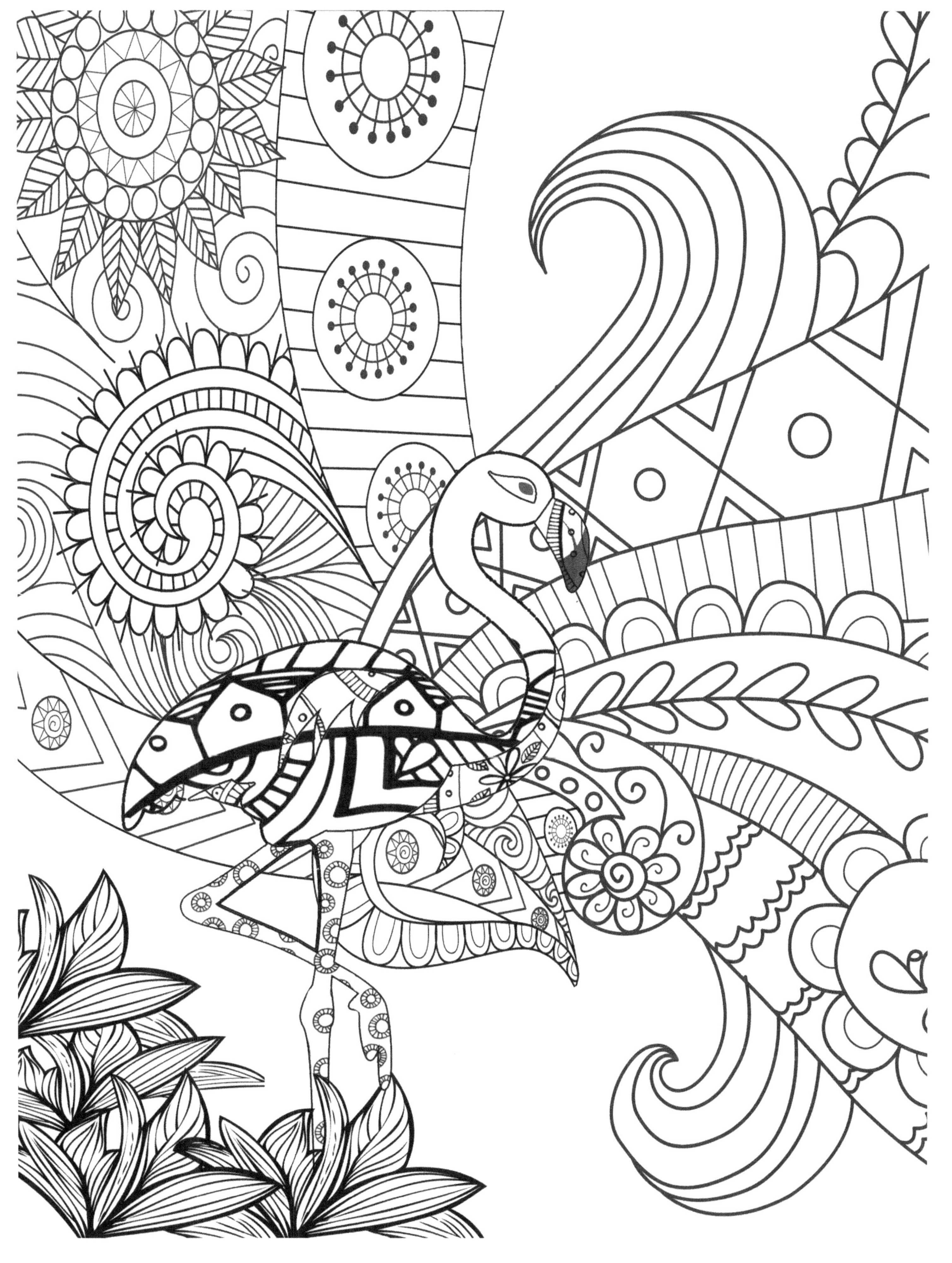

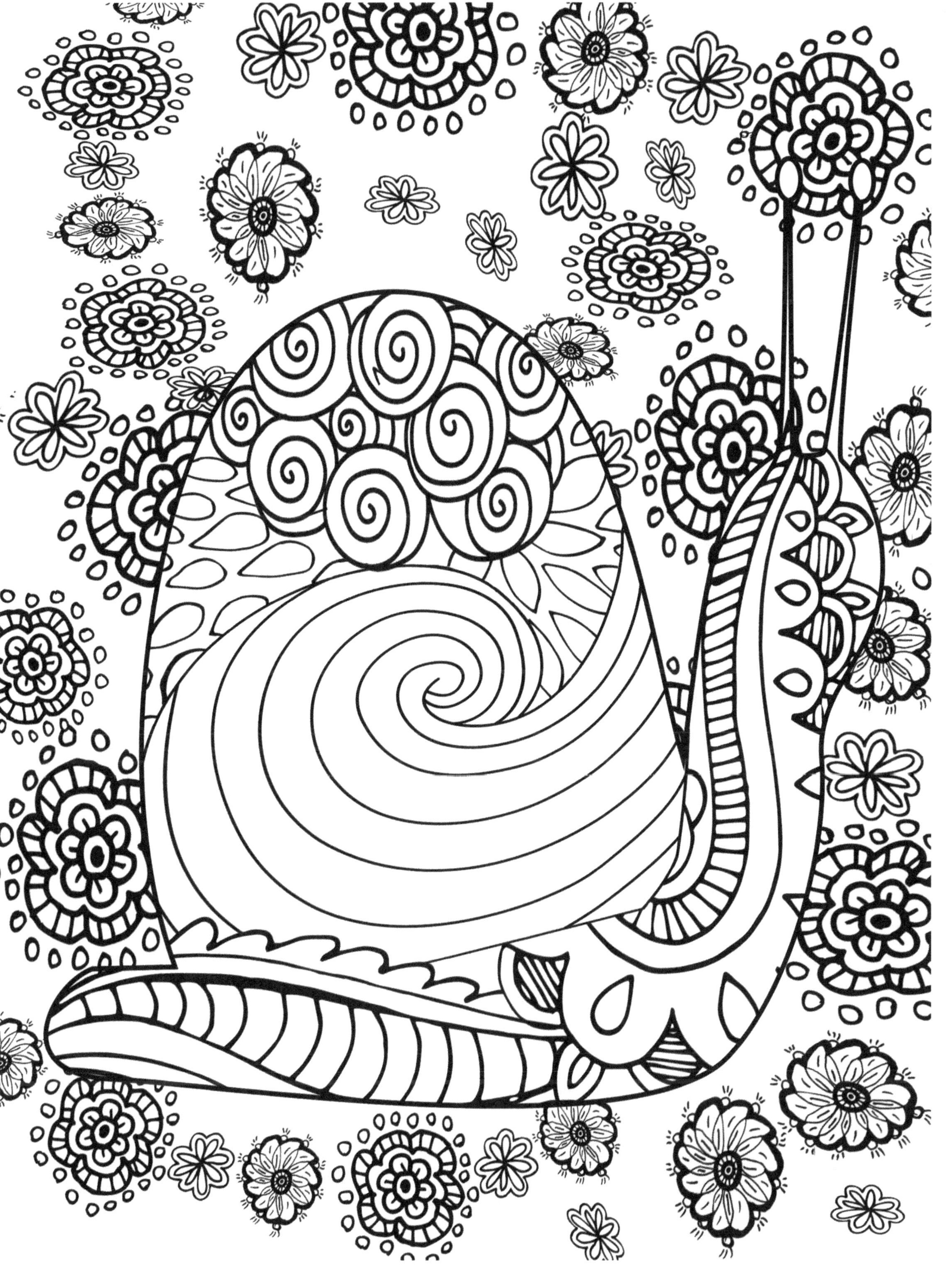

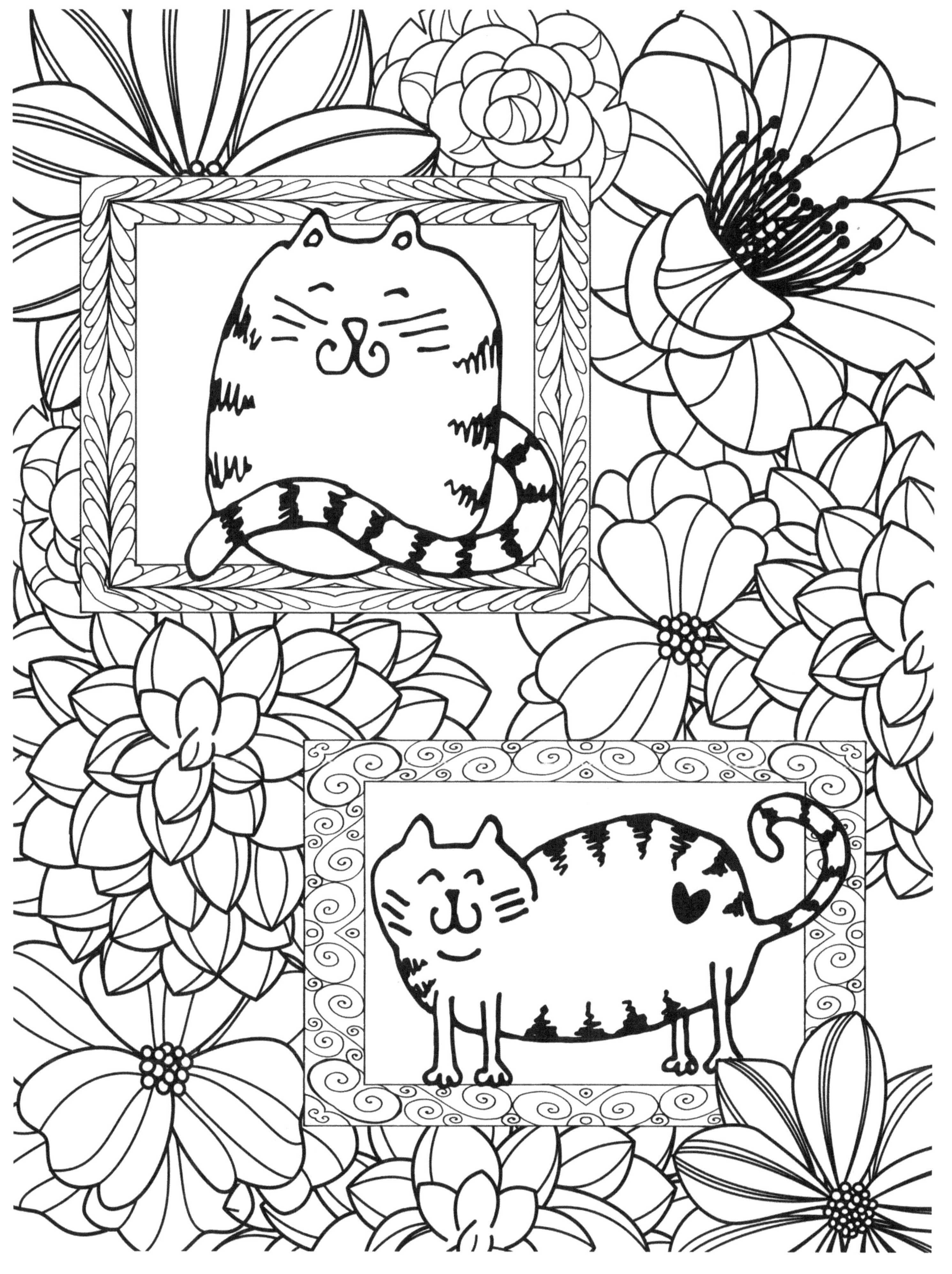